SUPER HUMANS!
GUINNESS
WORLD
RECORDS

by Donald Lemke

GUINNESS WORLD RECORDS: OFFICIALLY AMAZING

Since 1955, Guinness World Records has been the world's most trusted, accurate, and recognized source for record-breaking achievements. From the most bowling balls juggled to the most eggs crushed with toes to the fastest marathon dribbling a basketball, Guinness World Records is home to fascinating, zany, and breathtaking human feats, including the Officially Amazing records of these Super Humans.

Guinness World Records holders are truly amazing, but all attempts to set or break records are performed under controlled conditions and at the participant's own risk. Please seek out the appropriate guidance before you attempt any record-breaking activities.

Guinness World Records: Super Humans!
© 2016 Guinness World Records Limited
The words GUINNESS WORLD RECORDS and related logos
are trademarks of Guinness World Records Limited.
All records and information accurate as of August 1, 2015.
All rights reserved. Printed in the United States of America.
No part of this book may be used or reproduced in any manner
whatsoever without written permission except in the case of brief
quotations embodied in critical articles and reviews. For information
address HarperCollins Children's Books, a division of HarperCollins
Publishers, 195 Broadway, New York, NY 10007.
www.harpercollinschildrens.com

Library of Congress Control Number: 2015952904
ISBN 978-0-06-234173-0

Design by Victor Joseph Ochoa and Sean Boggs
15 16 17 18 19   PC/RRDC   10 9 8 7 6 5 4 3 2 1
❖
First Edition

SECTION ONE:

SKILL

Some people dedicate years of training and practice to perfect their amazing skills—people like Australian Chayne Hultgren (right), who has a way with swords!

In this section, discover more individuals committed to breaking records using their remarkable skills.

Where there's smoke, there's Hubertus Wawra. On February 21, 2011, in Mumbai, India, this German fire-eater **extinguished the most torches in 30 seconds** . . . with his mouth! His record-setting total is 39.

Canadian Trever McGhee achieved the **farthest fire-walking distance** when he strutted 597 feet barefoot over hot embers with a temperature between 1,214–1,307 degrees Fahrenheit in Alberta, Canada, on November 9, 2007.

GREAT BALLS OF FIRE!

On January 11, 2011, in Las Vegas, Nevada, Antonio Restivo blew the **highest flame ever by a fire breather**. He held a flammable fuel in his mouth and then blew the liquid onto a burning torch. The resulting fireball scorched a ceiling 26 feet, 5 inches above his head.

FARTHEST FIRE-WALKING DISTANCE TIMELINE:

June 15, 2005: Amanda Dennison (Canada) = 220 feet

January 28, 2006: Scott Bell (UK) = 250 feet

November 7, 2006: Trever McGhee (Canada) = 294 feet, 7 inches

November 28, 2006: Scott Bell = 328 feet

July 7, 2007: Trever McGhee = 389 feet

South African duo Enrico Schoeman and Andre De Kock share the record for the **longest motorcycle ride through a tunnel of fire**. They completed the fiery ride of 338 feet, 2.65 inches on a motorbike with a sidecar on August 10, 2012, in Vaalwater, Limpopo province, South Africa.

On September 3, 2004, Natasha Veruschka (pictured below with a light sword) achieved the **most swords swallowed simultaneously by a female** when she swallowed 13 swords down the hatch without a scratch! The feat was performed at the 3rd Annual Sideshow Gathering and Sword Swallowers Convention in Wilkes-Barre, Pennsylvania.

FACT!
The act of sword-swallowing began more than 4,000 years ago in India.

FOCUS ON: CHAYNE HULTGREN

Chayne, also known as the Space Cowboy, definitely lives by the sword. Born April 13, 1979, he is a popular and perilous performer from Byron Bay, Australia, and currently holds more Guinness World Records than any other Australian. His 13 current records center on sword-swallowing, juggling, knife-throwing, and a variety of other death-defying acts, including:

★ **Highest throw and catch of a chain saw while juggling**—11 feet, 9.3 inches

★ **Heaviest weight pulled with the eye sockets**—907 pounds

★ **Most chain saw–juggling catches on a unicycle**—8!

GULP!

Here's a record that's hard to swallow . . . On September 12, 2012, in London, UK, Chayne swallowed 24 swords, the **most swords swallowed simultaneously by a male**!

Sword-swallowing wasn't tricky enough for Chayne. He threw a unicycle into the mix. On November 15, 2012, he set the record for **most swords swallowed while on a unicycle**: 3. Now that's multitasking!

Alex Barron rarely drops the ball . . . even when he's juggling 11 of them! On April 3, 2012, Alex achieved the all-time record for **most balls juggled**. At the Roehampton Squash Club in London, he juggled 11 balls, managing 23 consecutive catches in total.

On the flip side, Czech juggling pro Zdeněk Bradáč holds the record for the **most balls juggled while suspended upside down**. On November 1, 2010, in Jablonec nad Nisou, Czech Republic, he successfully juggled four balls while hanging upside down, completing 20 consecutive catches. To set the record, the magician, juggler, and escapologist suspended himself by wearing gravity boots.

The **longest duration juggling three objects while suspended upside down** is 12 minutes, 50 seconds and was accomplished by Quinn Spicker of Canada at the PNE Garden Auditorium in Vancouver, British Columbia, Canada, on July 22, 2010.

Canadian Ian Stewart has a ball juggling his chain saws! On September 25, 2011, the entertainer achieved the **most chain saw–juggling catches**. He juggled three running chain saws for a total of 94 catches. One day, Ian hopes to break—or, saw through—his own record and reach 100 consecutive catches.

Milan Roskopf from Slovakia juggles a perfect game! On November 19, 2011, he achieved the record for **juggling the most bowling balls**. He kept three balls aloft—each weighing 10 pounds—at the Prague juggling marathon in the Czech Republic.

MORE JUGGLING ACTS:

The **most boomerangs juggled** is five, achieved by Danny Luftman in Ventimiglia, Italy, on December 29, 2013.

The **most under-leg chain saw–juggling passes by a team of two** is 40, achieved by Chayne Hultgren and Gareth Williams in Beijing, China, on December 7, 2012.

NASA pilot Donald E. Williams became the **first person to juggle in outer space**, while on board the space shuttle *Discovery* on April 15, 1985. He was able to juggle several pieces of fruit while in orbit.

RIGHT ON TARGET!

Breaking Peter Terry's record is definitely a *long* shot, to say the least. That's because the Australian holds the record for the **farthest accurate distance in men's archery**. Terry struck a 48-inch target positioned 656 feet, 2 inches away on December 15, 2005, in Perth, Western Australia, Australia.

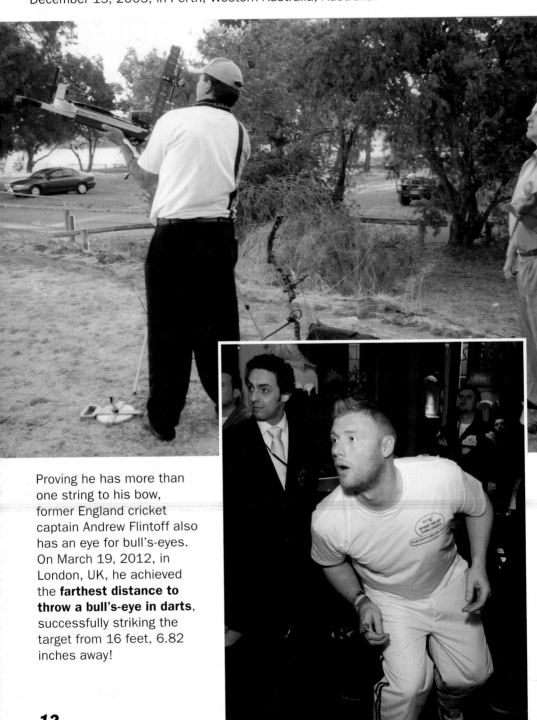

Proving he has more than one string to his bow, former England cricket captain Andrew Flintoff also has an eye for bull's-eyes. On March 19, 2012, in London, UK, he achieved the **farthest distance to throw a bull's-eye in darts**, successfully striking the target from 16 feet, 6.82 inches away!

FOCUS ON: DAVID ADAMOVICH

David Adamovich is the self-proclaimed World's Fastest and Most Accurate Knife Thrower. With 40 Guinness World Records set or broken, David's knife-throwing skills are hard to deny.

On December 26, 2007, David lobbed the **most knives thrown around a human target in one minute**. Also known as the Great Throwdini, he launched 102 throwing knives around his partner, Tina Nagy, in 60 seconds in Freeport, New York.

David sure lived up to his stage name! He surrounded his assistant with throwing knives in 4.29 seconds in Mexico on July 29, 2008—the **fastest time to throw 10 knives around a human target**.

CATCHING AIR!

The **highest jump through a hoop** is 10 feet, 2 inches. That's higher than a basketball hoop! Qiu Jiangning of China achieved the feat on the set of a Guinness World Records television special in Beijing, China, on June 17, 2009.

The **most bars jumped on the back wheel of a trial bike** is 48 and was achieved by Benito Ros Charral of Spain, on the set of *Lo Show dei Record,* in Milan, Italy, on April 19, 2009. Benito jumped from bar to bar in one direction; at the end of the structure he stopped on a small platform, turned around while remaining on the back wheel of the bicycle, and jumped back.

The **highest shallow dive** was from a height of 37 feet, 11 inches into 12 inches of water and was achieved by American Darren Taylor (aka Professor Splash) on the set of *CCTV Guinness World Records Special* in Xiamen, Fujian, China, on September 9, 2014.

OLLIE-OOP!

On February 15, 2011, in Las Vegas, Nevada, Aldrin Garcia achieved the **highest skateboard ollie** of all time. This trick consists of raising all four skateboard wheels off the ground simultaneously. Aldrin ollied 45 inches over a rigid high bar without making contact with any part of his body or board. Setting the record at only 19 years old, he has plenty of time to raise that bar again.

On May 12, 2012, Lisa Coolen set the record for the **highest unassisted martial arts kick by a female**— 7 feet, 8 inches!

Fred Fugen and Vince Reffet performed the **highest BASE jump from a building** at 2,716 feet, 6 inches off the Burj Khalifa tower in Dubai, United Arab Emirates, which currently holds its own record as the **tallest building in the world**. BASE stands for Building, Antenna, Span, and Earth. A BASE jumper leaps from any of these objects, deploying a parachute before reaching the ground.

Dalibor Jablanović from Serbia wasn't born with a silver spoon on his nose—learning that skill took practice! On September 28, 2013, in Stubica, Serbia, Dalibor achieved the all-time record for **most spoons balanced on the face**—a whopping 31!

TRY THIS AT HOME, KIDS!

Balancing a spoon on your nose can be a fun and easy party trick. Follow these instructions to learn a GWR skill!

- ★ Locate a metal spoon.
- ★ Breathe onto the scooping part of the spoon to moisten the metal.
- ★ Place the scooping part of the spoon on your nose.
- ★ Let go, and let the spoon hang!

THIRSTY?

John Evans has the answer. On June 5, 2007, in Derbyshire, UK, John balanced 429 drink cans on his head with a total weight of 381 pounds, 6 ounces. That's the **most drink cans balanced on the head**—and enough soda to quench anyone's thirst!

FACT!
John Evans's supersized neck is two feet around!

LOOK, MA, NO HANDS!

On October 22, 2011, in Dhaka, Bangladesh, Abdul Halim traveled 9.44 miles—the **farthest distance with a soccer ball balanced on the head**. That's the equivalent of more than 125 soccer fields!

Tatum Braun definitely knows how to strike a balance. On July 10, 2015, she achieved the **longest balance-board duration**: 7 hours, 25 minutes, 30.86 seconds in Charlotte, Vermont. Often used for exercise, balance boards create an unstable footing, forcing users to keep the edges of the board from rocking or touching the ground.

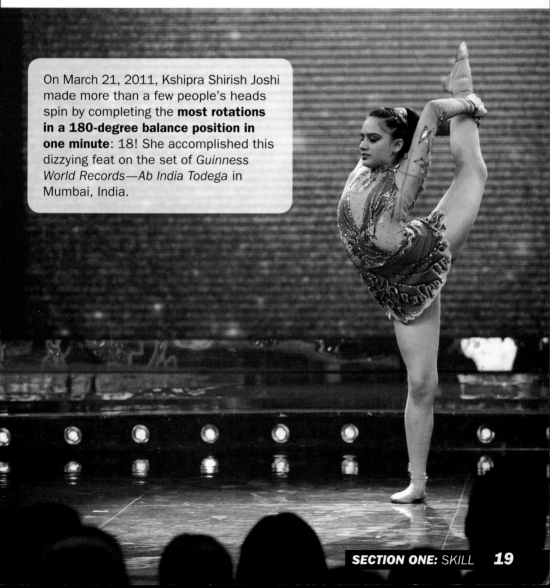

On March 21, 2011, Kshipra Shirish Joshi made more than a few people's heads spin by completing the **most rotations in a 180-degree balance position in one minute**: 18! She accomplished this dizzying feat on the set of *Guinness World Records—Ab India Todega* in Mumbai, India.

FOCUS ON: ASHRITA FURMAN

Ashrita Furman was born September 15, 1954, in Brooklyn, New York. He first made his way into Guinness World Records in 1979 by performing 27,000 jumping jacks. He holds more Guinness World Records titles than any other person—his count stood at 521 records as of 2014.

The **greatest distance walked by a person continuously balancing a milk bottle on the head** is 80.96 miles. Ashrita achieved this by walking around Victory Field track in Forest Park in Queens, from April 22 to 23, 1998. The feat took 23 hours, 35 minutes.

CHEERS!

On August 12, 2007, he balanced 81 pint (20-ounce) glasses on his chin for 12.10 seconds, the **most pint glasses balanced on the chin**!

Ashrita also holds the record for the **greatest distance traveled with a pool cue balanced on the chin**—5,472 feet, 9 inches! He set the record at Joe Austin Playground in Jamaica, New York, on July 6, 2008.

Right on cue, Ashrita broke another balancing record! On February 19, 2010, the perennial record-breaker achieved the record for the **farthest distance traveled with a pool cue balanced on the finger**, reaching an astonishing distance of 8.95 miles.

BALANCING ACT BONANZA:

The **highest tightrope crossed on a motorcycle** is 426 feet, 6.12 inches in height and 2,185 feet, 4.32 inches in length, achieved by Mustafa Danger in Benidorm, Spain, on October 16, 2010.

The **longest tightrope crossing by bicycle** is 235 feet, by American Nik Wallenda in Newark, New Jersey, on October 15, 2008.

The **most 360-degree spins on a tightrope in two minutes** is 41, by Maimaitiaili Abula on the set of *CCTV—Guinness World Records Special* in Beijing, China, on September 20, 2007.

Mike Howard isn't full of hot air . . . he truly did set the record for **highest altitude for a balloon skywalk**! On September 1, 2004, near Yeovil, Somerset, UK, Howard walked on a beam between two balloons at an altitude of 21,400 feet as part of a recording for the *Guinness World Records: 50 Years, 50 Records* television show.

MORE BALLOON BREAKERS:

Dr. Vijaypat Singhania of India piloted the **highest flight by a balloon**, reaching 68,986 feet in a Cameron Z-1600 hot-air balloon over Mumbai, India, on November 26, 2005.

The **fastest skywalk between two hot-air balloons** is 7.49 seconds and was achieved by Freddy Nock of Switzerland on October 4, 2014. He took those speedy steps on the set of *CCTV-Guinness World Records Special* in Tangshan Ziqing Lake Eco-tourism Hot Spring Resort, Nanjing, Jiangsu, China. The sure-footed tightrope walker also holds the record for **longest cable walk**, traveling 3,624 feet up a cable-car wire in Germany in 2009.

On July 27, 2004, in Ottumwa, Iowa, Emma Carrol became the **oldest person to fly in a hot-air balloon**. Born May 18, 1895, Carrol accomplished the feat at the age of 109 years, 70 days.

Reymond Adina deserves an awful big tip! On October 24, 2007, at the Quatre-Gats restaurant in Barcelona, Spain, the waiter broke the record for the **most wine glasses held in one hand**—39! The number of glasses held in the hand is a matter of pride for Barcelona's waiters. Many are able to carry dozens of glasses without breaking them, but Reymond is the best of the best.

On June 23, 2009, in Las Vegas, Nevada, Erik Skramstad achieved the **longest distance cycled in one hour without hands**. He traveled 23.25 miles.

For most people, this record might be too hard to handle. Not for French cycling circus performer Ivan Do-Duc! On April 14, 2011, in Milan, Italy, he coasted into the record books for the **longest time standing on the handlebars of a bicycle**—1 minute, 39.49 seconds.

On November 12, 2008, in New York City, Rob Beaton ate 23 grains of rice using chopsticks in one minute. Picking up each grain one by one, Rob consumed the **most rice eaten in one minute**.

KNOCK, KNOCK
Who's there? Orange. Orange who? Orange you glad you know this record? The **most oranges peeled and eaten in three minutes** is 6, achieved first by Ashrita Furman (left) in 2010, then matched by Dinesh Upadhyaya of India in 2014.

In 2010, Ashrita Furman (right) achieved another sweet record, claiming the title for **most jelly eaten with chopsticks in one minute**—1 pound, 5 ounces. Think that sounds a lot? Well, he has since been beaten by Cherry Yoshitake of Japan, who ate 1 pound, 6 ounces of jelly in July 2014.

Speed-eater Takeru Kobayashi sure had a ball in New York City on March 8, 2010, when he consumed the **most meatballs eaten in one minute**: 29!

To achieve his record, Paul E. Lyday III went to grape lengths. On September 7, 2009, in Motte, South Carolina, he set the record for the **greatest distance a thrown grape has been caught in the mouth**—354 feet, 4 inches. That's longer than a football field! The grape was launched using a pouch attached to two elastic bands.

GRAPE MINDS THINK ALIKE!

On September 13, 2008, in Cologne, Germany, Martina Servaty achieved another grape-related record. She extracted the **most juice from grapes by stomping in two minutes**. Martina extracted 5.36 gallons of juice using only her feet.

26

Stephen Clarke sure knows how to carve up a happy Halloween! On October 29, 2008, he carved 2,205 pounds of pumpkins in 3 hours, 33 minutes, 49 seconds—the **fastest time to carve one ton of pumpkins**—in Atlantic City, New Jersey. That's a lot of jack-o'-lanterns!

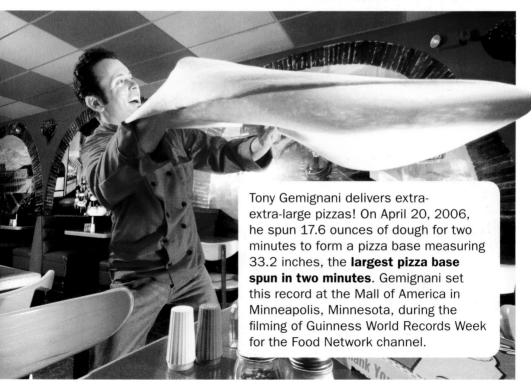

Tony Gemignani delivers extra-extra-large pizzas! On April 20, 2006, he spun 17.6 ounces of dough for two minutes to form a pizza base measuring 33.2 inches, the **largest pizza base spun in two minutes**. Gemignani set this record at the Mall of America in Minneapolis, Minnesota, during the filming of Guinness World Records Week for the Food Network channel.

Ashrita Furman knows how to scramble an egg—with his toes! On June 5, 2012, in New York City, he achieved the record for the **most eggs crushed with the toes in one minute**, scrambling 55 of them! Or, in egg terms, about four and a half dozen.

The **most eggs crushed with the toes in 30 seconds** is 39 and was also achieved by Ashrita at the Sri Chinmoy Centre in Jamaica, New York, on November 21, 2012.

EGG-CELLENT ACHIEVEMENTS:

The **fastest time to balance a dozen eggs** is 1 minute, 6.45 seconds, achieved by Brian Spotts at Legacy Elementary in Frederick, Colorado, on February 6, 2015. Brian discovered he had a knack for balancing eggs while at college.

The **fastest time to eat three pickled eggs** is 34.50 seconds, set by Kyle Thomas Moyer in Coopersburg, Pennsylvania, on November 19, 2013.

The **most eggs cracked in one hour with one hand** is 3,031, by Corey Perras (above) at the Broadway Bar & Grill, Barrhaven, Ontario, Canada, on June 22, 2012. All 3,031 successfully cracked eggs along with hash browns and sausages were donated to the Ottawa Mission for a large weekend breakfast feast.

The path to a Guinness World Records title isn't always smooth—sometimes it's a rocky road! On September 1, 2007, German duo Gabriele Soravia (thrower) and Lorenzo Soravia (catcher) achieved the record for **most ice-cream scoops thrown and caught in one minute by a team**: 25! Now that's a sweet success.

This next record is udder madness! On September 1, 2004, Ilker Yilmaz from Turkey fired milk from his eye a distance of 9 feet, 2 inches, setting a new record for **farthest distance to squirt milk**.

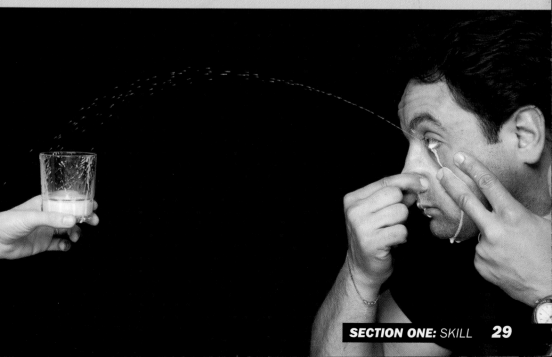

Ashrita Furman never runs out of juice! On November 2, 2007, he recorded the **fastest time to push an orange one mile using the nose**. He completed the sweet feat in 22 minutes, 41 seconds in Valley Stream, New York.

DOUBLE THE BUBBLE!

Here are two bubble-gum records to chew on:

On April 24, 2004, in Winston County, Alabama, Chad Fell blew a bubble-gum bubble with a diameter of 20 inches. He created the **largest bubble-gum bubble blown** without using his hands.

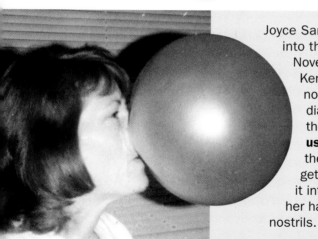

Joyce Samuels nosed her way into the record books on November 10, 2000. In Louisville, Kentucky, she blew from her nose a bubble-gum bubble with a diameter of 11 inches, achieving the **largest bubble-gum bubble using the nose**. Samuels chews the gum for at least an hour to get the sugar out before making it into a rectangle shape with her hands and putting it over her nostrils.

BUBBLE BREAKERS:

The **most bubble-gum bubbles blown in one minute** is 15, achieved by Michael Amato of New Jersey on September 14, 2014.

The **most people blowing a chewing gum bubble simultaneously** is 737 and was achieved by global confectioner ChupaChups at Joy Eslava in Madrid, Spain, on September 27, 2014. This beat the previous record by 16 people!

FOOD FOR THOUGHT:

The **most watermelons chopped on the stomach in one minute** is 48 and was achieved by Bipin Larkin and Ashrita Furman at the Sri Chinmoy Centre in Jamaica, New York, on November 30, 2012.

On January 8, 2014, Lee Moon Ky of South Korea was on a roll! He broke the record for the **most pizza rolls across the shoulders in 30 seconds**, rolling 38 rounds of pizza dough across his shoulders in Jiangsu, China.

Italian Maurizio Paschetta squeezed into the Guinness World Records book with the **most milk extracted from a cow in two minutes**. On May 26, 2012, in Saluzzo, Cuneo, Italy, he extracted 7.91 pints to achieve the record. Paschetta comes from four generations of farmers, and he decided to attempt this record to show the importance of work and tradition. In fact, he milks his cows every day without using any mechanical devices.

THE TOP OF HIS GAME!

The **most golf balls driven into a target area from the knees in 12 hours** is 2,575, achieved by Brian Lovegren in Buckeye, Arizona, on December 20, 2011.

On January 7, 2010, Ashrita Furman broke into an exclusive club. He earned the Guinness World Records title for the **longest control of a golf ball with one club**. Using a Wilson Sandy Andy sand wedge club, he controlled the ball for 1 hour, 20 minutes, 42 seconds at the Panorama Café in New York City.

Golfer Kermit Dannehl is certainly good at his long game. Between 1992 and 2007, Dannehl achieved the record for the **most times a golfer scored their age and below**: 1,138. Most of these scores were recorded at Ahwatukee Country Club, Phoenix, Arizona.

TENNIS, ANYONE?

The **most tennis balls caught in one hour** is 904, achieved by Anthony Kelly of Australia at Armidale City Bowling Club in Armidale, New South Wales, Australia, on November 13, 2011.

The **most tennis serves in one hour** is an amazing 1,158! Sean Rooney of Ireland served up this record at the County Wicklow Lawn Tennis Club, Bray, Ireland, on September 18, 2011. Serves were only counted if they landed within the lines.

TOP TENNIS RECORDS:

The **most alternate hits with a tennis racket in one minute** is 75, achieved by Toru Suzuki of Japan at Tokyo Midtown, in Minato, Tokyo, on April 29, 2015. He also shares the 30-second record for the same feat.

The **most tennis balls held in the hand** is 23 and was achieved by Mahadeo Bhujbal of India in Pune, Maharashtra, India, on September 8, 2013.

Andy Macdonald is X-tremely good at skateboarding. He holds the record for the **most ESPN Summer X Games Skateboard medals** at 23, as of 2013. Macdonald took home his first-ever medal in 1999.

FOCUS ON: ANDY MACDONALD

Andy Macdonald was born in Boston, Massachusetts, on July 31, 1973. He was given his first skateboard at the age of 12 and was immediately hooked, teaching himself two or three new tricks every day. Andy competed in the X Games for the first time in 1995 and by 1999 had won eight medals and was named Overall World Cup Skateboarding Champion. When he's not skating, Andy acts as a spokesman for the Partnership for a Drug-Free America.

On August 1, 2009, Ivan Sebastian Cordova achieved the **most nollies in 30 seconds**, 15, at X Games 15 in Los Angeles, California.

A day later, on August 2, 2009, Sten Carr set the record for the **most ollies completed in 30 seconds**, 34, at the same event, X Games 15, in Los Angeles, California.

FACT!

Nollies and ollies are skateboarding tricks where all four wheels of a skateboard are raised off the flat ground simultaneously. In an ollie, a skateboarder pops the board up at the tail with their back foot. And in a nollie, the skateboarder's front foot does the work, popping up the nose of the skateboard first.

Taïg Khris is leaps and bounds above the competition! On May 29, 2010, during the M6 Mobile Mega Jump event in Paris, France, he achieved the record for the **highest inline-skate drop into a half pipe** at 41 feet.

WHAT A RUSH!

On June 18, 2012, Canadian Mischo Erban broke the record for the **fastest skateboard speed, standing**. He achieved a speed of 80.74 miles per hour at Les Éboulements, Quebec, Canada.

The **first person to perform a 1080 on a skateboard** is Tom Schaar. The skateboarder achieved the feat by completing three full rotations in the air, using an extra-large half pipe called a "mega ramp" at Woodward West, Tehachapi, California, on March 26, 2012.

The **highest wall ride on a skateboard** is 7 feet, 6 inches, achieved by Brad Edwards and Aaron Murray at the *Juice Magazine*—USSA WSA—The Board Gallery—Hollywood Skate Jam in Hollywood, California, on August 25, 2006.

MORE XTREME FEATS:

Skateboard legend Tony Hawk became the **first person to achieve a 900**—two and a half airborne rotations on a skateboard—in competition at the ESPN X Games 5 in San Francisco, California, on June 27, 1999.

The **most consecutive kick flips on a skateboard** is 1,546 and was achieved by Zach Kral at 4 Seasons Skate Park, Milwaukee, Wisconsin, on November 30, 2008.

The **longest dirt-to-dirt mountain bike backflip** is 100 feet, 3 inches and was achieved by Cam Zink at the ESPN World of X Games: Mammoth Flip Presented by Monster Energy at Mammoth Mountain's Canyon Lodge in Mammoth Lakes, California, on August 21, 2014.

The **longest ollie on a snowskate board** is 11 feet, 4 inches, by Phil Smage at ESPN's Winter X Games 11 in Aspen, Colorado, on January 27, 2007.

The **most BMX Freestyle medals won at the Summer X Games** is 23 and was achieved by Dave Mirra from 1995 to 2011. Until recently, Mirra held the overall record for **most Summer X Games medals won** across all disciplines with 24, but Bob Burnquist of Brazil now holds the record with 27.

The **most 360-degree front-side spins on a skateboard in 30 seconds** is six, by Lunati Hamilton at X Games 15 in Los Angeles, California, on July 30, 2009.

Some say Hula-Hooping is a *waist* of time! Gregory Sean Dillon of California does not agree. On March 20, 2010, he broke the record for the **most revolutions of a Hula-Hoop in one minute**—243!

Willi Maier of Austria hit the nail on the head for his record—actually, he hit two dozen of them! On September 26, 2010, in Vienna, Maier achieved the **most nails hammered into a block of wood in one minute** with a total of 24. He nailed it!

HI-YA!

The **most martial-arts sword cuts in one minute** is 68, achieved by Konstantinos Karipidis of Greece in Alexandroupolis, on May 28, 2011.

NOW YOU SEE IT . . .

Now you don't, and neither did Fernando Diaz of Venezuela (pictured). On August 17, 2011, on the set of the live television show *Buenas Noches* in Caracas, the magician performed the **most magic tricks while blindfolded in one minute**—17! More amazing still, he has been surpassed by Clive Greenaway of the UK, who performed 18 tricks in June 2015.

On July 23, 2015, Stephen Rainey of the UK spun his way into the record books, all in support of a great cause! He achieved the **most manual wheelchair spins in one minute**, 66, at an event in Liverpool, UK, that raised awareness of assistance available to local residents requiring wheelchair services.

HEADS UP!

The **most headers of a ball while tightrope walking in one minute** is 101, achieved by Russian Mikhail Ivanov in Ivanovo, Russia, on September 18, 2012.

This next record would be a pain in the neck for most, but not for Ashrita Furman! He achieved the **most basketball neck catches in one minute**, 27, in New York City on October 2, 2009.

At first glance, you might think this record is just toilet humor, but Gerhard Donie of Germany is deadly serious about record-breaking. In 2010, he achieved the record for **most human targets hit with plungers in one minute**: 15!

The world record for **most lasso Texas skips in one minute** is 80, accomplished by Daniel Ledda of Spain, on the set of *Guinness World Records—El Show de los Records* in Madrid, on June 11, 2006. A Texas skip involves twirling a lasso in a vertical loop on one side of the body and then jumping sideways back and forth through the loop.

NICE KICKS!

The **most touches of a soccer ball in one minute by a female**, while keeping the ball in the air, is 339, by Chloe Hegland from Canada. She performed the feat on the set of *Zheng Da Zong Yi—Guinness World Records Special* in Beijing, China, on November 3, 2007.

Manuel Torres achieved the **most wheelie hops in 30 seconds**, 62, at X Games 15 in Los Angeles, California, on August 30, 2009. A wheelie hop consists of lifting only the front wheel of a bicycle off the ground.

Bryan Ventura is the wheel deal! At the same X Games and on the same day, he set the record for the **most bunny hops on a BMX bicycle in 30 seconds**: 41. A bunny hop, in this instance, consists of lifting both wheels of the bicycle off the ground.

The **most drink cans broken with a whip in three minutes** is 23, achieved by Adam Winrich of the United States on the set of *Lo Show dei Record*, in Milan, Italy, on April 11, 2009. To perform this feat, he used a bullwhip, a type of rawhide whip with a long, braided lash.

On January 25, 2003, in Jerome, Idaho, Kimberly Mink recorded the **largest trick-roping loop by a female**. She spun the loop around her, fed to a length of 76 feet, 2 inches, measured from the end of the eye of the rope to her hand.

YEE-HAW!

The record for the **largest trick-roping loop by a male** was achieved by Charlie Keyes, who spun a loop around him fed to a length of 107 feet, 2 inches. He performed the feat on April 22, 2006, at the Will Rogers International Wild West Expo in Claremore, Oklahoma.

John Cassidy doesn't clown around! He holds the record for the **most modeling balloon sculptures made in one hour**. On November 14, 2007, he made 747 balloon shapes in 60 minutes at Bucks County Community College in Newtown, Pennsylvania.

Kurt Steiner made a real splash with his record—or, make that a ripple! He set the record for the **most consecutive skips of a stone on water**—88—at Red Bridge, near Kane, Pennsylvania, on September 6, 2013.

The **most spears caught from a spear gun underwater in one minute** is 10, captured by Anthony Kelly of Australia in a sports center swimming pool on November 13, 2014. As the rules state, Kelly had to stand no closer than 6 feet, 6 inches from the shooter during the attempt.

The **most spears caught from a spear gun above water in one minute** is 13 and was achieved by Ashrita Furman in New York City, on July 17, 2014.

SECTION TWO:
STRENGTH

Strength of both body and mind have led
many to greatness—and Guinness World
Records! In this section, read all about the
individuals who lifted themselves above the rest.

SMAAASH!

This record attempt by Turkish strongman Ali Bahçetepe was a smashing success! On November 17, 2012, in Datça Cumhuriyet Meydani, Turkey, he achieved the **most concrete blocks broken in one minute**—1,175!

Davide Cenciarelli from Italy is another smash hit, or at least he should be! On March 18, 2010, he set the record for the **most watermelons smashed with a fist in one minute** with 70.

On June, 2, 2012, Jemal Tkeshelashvili of Georgia set the record for the **most hot-water bottles burst with the nose in one minute** when he blasted through three water bottles!

This record would be hard for anyone to break, er, burst—except Shaun Jones of the UK. On March 31, 2011, in Milan, Italy, Jones set the record for **fastest time to blow up a standard hot-water bottle until it bursts**. He achieved the amazing feat in 6.52 seconds.

HOT-WATER BOTTLE BREAKERS:

The **fastest time to blow up a standard hot-water bottle until it bursts by a female** is 41.20 seconds, achieved by Shobha S. Tipnis in Mumbai, India, on March 17, 2011.

The **fastest time to burst three hot-water bottles** is 28.82 seconds, by Shaun Jones at Hope House Children's Hospice, Oswestry, Shropshire, UK, on November 17, 2011, in celebration of Guinness World Records Day.

The **most hot-water bottles burst in one minute** is five, by Brian Jackson on the set of *Guinness World Records Gone Wild!* in Los Angeles, California, on July 6, 2012.

Aneta Florczyk from Poland doesn't throw her own weight around—she throws other people's weight around! On December 19, 2008, in Madrid, Spain, she achieved the record for the **most people lifted and thrown in two minutes**, with 12 individuals tossed.

"TIMBERRRR!"

American Erin Lavoie is certainly familiar with this lumberjack phrase. On December 19, 2008, in Germany, Lavoie chopped down the **most Christmas trees in two minutes**: 27. Just in time for the holidays!

The **most bowls broken with one finger in one minute** is 102, achieved by Fan Weipeng of China. After setting the record on April 11, 2009, in Milan, Italy, Weipeng needed a break from breaking!

When it comes to breaking records, James Thompson of the United States jumps right in! On June 9, 2010, in Tokyo, Japan, he achieved the **greatest weight supported while skipping rope 10 times**. He bore three people with a combined weight of 407.8 pounds during the incredible feat.

On May 24, 1999, in London, UK, John Evans balanced a gutted Mini car weighing a total of 352 pounds on his head for 33 seconds. This feat set the all-time record for the **heaviest car balanced on the head**.

John also achieved the **heaviest weight balanced on the head**—416 pounds using 101 bricks! He held the mighty load for 10 seconds in London, UK, on December 24, 1997.

MORE RECORDS BY JOHN EVANS:

Most milk crates balanced on the head—96

Tallest column of books balanced on the head—73 inches

Most beer kegs balanced on the head—11

The **most car-door windows smashed using fists in two minutes** is 21, set by American Kevin Taylor on the set of *Rekorlar Dünyasi* in Istanbul, Turkey, on June 26, 2013. Hopefully Taylor has good car insurance!

On September 7, 2009, strongman Kevin Fast of Canada pulled a CC-177 Globemaster III plane, weighing 416,299 pounds (188.83 tons). By going a distance of 28 feet, 10.46 inches at Canadian Forces Base in Ontario, he achieved the record for the **heaviest aircraft ever pulled by a man**!

Paddy Doyle breaks records with one hand behind his back! On November 27, 1993, in Sparkbrook, UK, he achieved the record for the **most one-arm push-ups completed in one hour**—a whopping 1,868!

On the other hand, Xie Guizhong of China is breaking records with just one finger! He completed the **most one-finger push-ups in 30 seconds**, 41, on the set of *CCTV—Guinness World Records Special* in Beijing on December 8, 2011.

Mohammed Mohammed Ali Zeinhom wasn't letting this record slip through his fingers! The Egyptian strongman achieved the **most two-finger push-ups (one arm) in one minute**, 46, in front of the Giza Pyramids in Cairo on March 8, 2010.

The **most one-arm push-ups on the back of the hand in one hour** is 1,025, achieved by Canadian Doug Pruden at the Don Wheaton Family YMCA in Edmonton, Alberta, on November 8, 2008.

MORE PUSH-UP RECORDS:

The **most knuckle push-ups in one minute** is 58, achieved by Bobby Natoli at the Pacific Health Club in Liverpool, New York, on March 22, 2014.

Paddy Doyle performed the **most one-arm push-ups in five hours**: 8,794. He accomplished this feat at Stamina's Kickboxing Self Defence Gym in Birmingham, West Midlands, UK, on February 12, 1996.

The **most push-ups on the back of the hands in one minute carrying a 40-pound pack** is 51, achieved by Patrick Hardy at In-Shape City, in Lompoc, California, on April 13, 2013.

Kevin Fast of Canada knows there's no place like home—so he took one with him! On September 18, 2010, in Ontario, he achieved the record for the **heaviest house pulled by an individual**. He moved the house, weighing 79,145 pounds, a distance of 39 feet, 2.47 inches.

They say loose lips sink ships, but good teeth will pull them! On November 9, 2001, in Makhachkala, Russia, Omar Hanapiev achieved the record for the **heaviest ship pulled by teeth**, moving a 1,269,861-pound (576-ton) tanker a distance of 49 feet, 2.4 inches. Hanapiev used a rope connected only to his superstrong gnashers.

RECORDS WITH BITE

Velue Rathakrishnan fought tooth and nail—but mostly tooth—to set the record for the **heaviest train pulled by teeth**! Rathakrishnan used his gnashers to pull two commuter trains, with a total weight of 574,964 pounds (260.8 tons), a distance of 13 feet, 9 inches along rails at Kuala Lumpur Railway Station in Malaysia on October 18, 2003.

The **heaviest road vehicle pulled with teeth** was a bus weighing 30,233.31 pounds and was achieved by Igor Zaripov of Russia on the set of *CCTV—Guinness World Records Special* in Jiangyin, Jiangsu, China on January 7, 2015.

The **greatest weight balanced on the teeth** is 140 pounds, achieved by Frank Simon, who supported a refrigerator on his gnashers for 10 seconds on May 17, 2007. At left is a previous attempt by Simon; to date, he has broken his own record six times!

Here's a record that'll put a lump in anyone's throat. On October 28, 2008, in Las Vegas, Nevada, Ryan Stock set the record for the **heaviest vehicle pulled by a swallowed sword**—3,740 pounds!

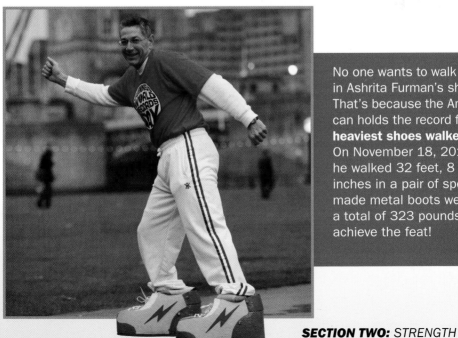

No one wants to walk a mile in Ashrita Furman's shoes! That's because the American holds the record for the **heaviest shoes walked in**. On November 18, 2010, he walked 32 feet, 8 inches in a pair of specially made metal boots weighing a total of 323 pounds to achieve the feat!

In addition to planes and houses, Kevin Fast also hauls fire trucks. The Canadian strongman holds the record for the **heaviest vehicle pulled over a level 100-foot course**. On September 15, 2008, Fast pulled a vehicle weighing a whopping 126,200 pounds on the television show *Live with Regis and Kelly* in New York City.

WHY PULL A CAR WHEN YOU CAN CARRY IT?

The **greatest distance carrying a car in one hour** is 1,337 feet, 7 inches, achieved by Mark Anglesea at Herringthorpe Running Track, Rotherham, UK, on October 2, 2010.

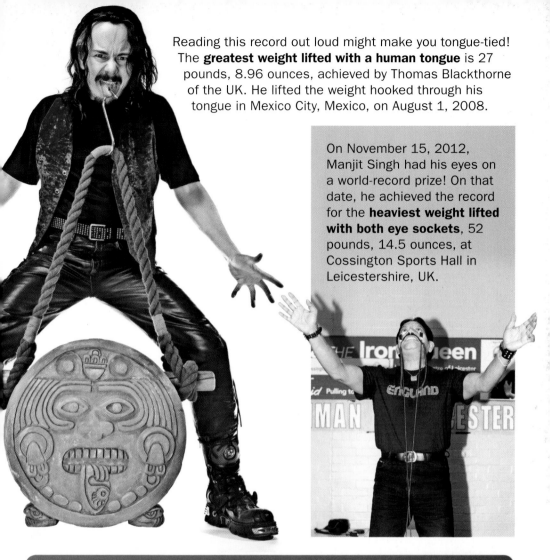

Reading this record out loud might make you tongue-tied! The **greatest weight lifted with a human tongue** is 27 pounds, 8.96 ounces, achieved by Thomas Blackthorne of the UK. He lifted the weight hooked through his tongue in Mexico City, Mexico, on August 1, 2008.

On November 15, 2012, Manjit Singh had his eyes on a world-record prize! On that date, he achieved the record for the **heaviest weight lifted with both eye sockets**, 52 pounds, 14.5 ounces, at Cossington Sports Hall in Leicestershire, UK.

EYE ON THE PRIZE:

The **heaviest car pulled by the eyelids** weighed 3,307 pounds and was pulled for 33 feet by Dong Changsheng of China through ropes hooked on his lower eyelids in Changchun, on September 26, 2006.

The **heaviest weight lifted with one eye socket by a female** is 13.23 pounds and was achieved by Asha Rani of India—also known as the Iron Queen—in Mahilpur, Punjab, on February 1, 2013.

Rani also holds the title for **heaviest weight lifted with both eye sockets by a female**—33 pounds, 6.4 ounces—achieved in Leicester, Leicestershire, UK, on February 12, 2014.

The **most accumulative weight bench-pressed in one hour** is 305,300 pounds. Irish weightlifter Eamonn Keane set this record at World Gym, Marina del Rey, California, on July 22, 2003.

The **heaviest weighted pull-up** was 206 pounds, 3.2 ounces, achieved by Steven Proto at a personal gym in Edmond, Oklahoma, on July 9, 2011.

On December 31, 2010, a lot hung in the balance for Ashrita Furman. On that date, he achieved the record for the **longest time to stand on a Swiss ball**: 5 hours, 7 minutes, 6 seconds, at the Panorama Café in New York City.

Ali Bahçetepe broke his own Guinness World Records title by breaking blocks. On March 18, 2015, he achieved the all-time record for the **most concrete blocks broken in a single stack**, 37, in Mugla, Turkey.

On November 9, 2008, in Saint Petersburg, Russian Alexander Muromskiy achieved the **fastest time to bend a 19-foot, 6-inch-long iron bar and fit it into a suitcase**. He accomplished the task in only 25 seconds. Let's hope he remembered to pack his toothbrush, too!

FOCUS ON: MANJIT SINGH

Born in March 1950, Manjit Singh, also known as the Iron Man of Leicester, moved to the UK to get married in 1977. He had been living in New Delhi, India, working for the police. In India, he used to lift stones in his spare time, which probably influenced his first Guinness World Records attempt. In 1987, he achieved the record for bench-pressing a weight of 56 pounds 1,035 times in one hour. Manjit holds several records, all of which involve the demonstration of great strength and stamina. He enjoys setting records not only for a sense of personal achievement, but because he raises a lot of money for charity at the same time.

Manjit can pull his own weight—and then some! He achieved the record for the **farthest distance to pull a single-decker bus with the ears**. On March 31, 2008, he pulled the bus 20 feet, raising money for the Manjit Fitness Academy in Loughborough, UK.

The **farthest distance to pull a double-decker bus with the hair** is 69.55 feet; Manjit achieved it in Battersea Park, London, UK, for Guinness World Records Day on November 11, 2009.

This record will blow your socks off. If it doesn't, Manjit will! He holds the record for the **most powerful lungs**. To prove it, he inflated a standard meteorological balloon to a diameter of 8 feet in 42 minutes at Rushley Pavilion Centre, Leicester, UK, on September 16, 1998.

FOCUS ON: WIM HOF

Born in 1959, Wim Hof of Finland has been involved in extreme outdoor activities for more than 25 years, including rock climbing, canyoneering, waterfall climbing, and ice diving. He makes use of meditation and yoga to overcome the dangers inherent in these activities, using breathing techniques to optimize his levels of concentration. He uses the "inner fire" yoga technique to regulate his body temperature and keep it at a normal 98.6 degrees Fahrenheit, even in extreme cold. Wim is planning four new record attempts: climbing Mont Blanc barefoot; spending four minutes under an ice floe without oxygen or protective clothing; spending an hour in an ice block–filled cylinder wearing just swimming trunks; and running 170 miles within the Arctic Circle without shoes and wearing just shorts.

Breaking records gives Wim Hof cold feet. On January 26, 2007, near Oulu, Finland, he achieved the **fastest half marathon while barefoot on ice or snow**: 2 hours, 16 minutes, 34 seconds. Let's hope he celebrated with a warm bath!

The **most bottle caps removed with the teeth in one minute** is 68. Murali K.C. of India achieved the feat at Country Club Mysore, in Bangalore, on September 17, 2011.

The **fastest 100-meter light aircraft pull** was 29.84 seconds, achieved by Montystar Agarawal of India on the set of *Guinness World Records—Ab India Todega* in Baramati, Maharashtra, on February 23, 2011.

The **longest distance walked while carrying a 10-pound brick** is 80.37 miles. Wearing no gloves, fitness fanatic Paddy Doyle of the UK achieved the feat in Warwickshire, on May 21, 2009.

Georges Christen of Luxembourg doesn't need dinner reservations—he just carries a table with him! On June 19, 2009, Christen achieved the **fastest 10 meters** (32 feet, 8 inches) **carrying a table with weight in the mouth**, 6.57 seconds. He also holds the record for **longest distance keeping a table lifted with the teeth**: 38 feet, 8 inches.

The **greatest weight lifted in one hour by kettlebell snatch for a female** is 31,614 pounds, 4.65 ounces and was achieved by Lyubov Cherepaha of Ukraine in Arkhangelsk, Russia, on June 23, 2014.

Jayanth Reddy of India is hardly the new kid on the block. . . . He holds the world record for smashing them! On July 29, 2012, in Hyderabad, Andhra Pradesh, Reddy achieved the **most concrete blocks broken using the roundhouse kick method in one minute**, 34.

With his trusty axe in hand, keen timber sportsman Robert Ebner from Germany rarely misses his target. The **most wooden logs chopped in half with one strike in one minute** is 70. Ebner chopped his way to the record on a German TV show on November 23, 2007.

The **most weight squat-lifted in 24 hours by an individual** is 1,013,350 pounds, 6 ounces, achieved by Shaun Jones of the UK at the Esporta Health Club in Norwich, on March 23, 2010. This attempt also made Jones the first man ever to lift a million pounds in 24 hours, a target he set himself and which will be hard to beat!

CHA! CHA! CHA!

The **oldest female acrobatic salsa dancer** is Sarah Paddy Jones of the UK, born July 1, 1934. She won the first prize on the Spanish television talent show *Tu Si Que Vales* in December 2009.

The **oldest competitive female bodybuilder** is E. Wilma Conner, born September 5, 1935. She last competed in the 2011 NPC Armbrust Pro Gym Warrior Classic Bodybuilding Championships in Loveland, Colorado, on August 20, 2011, at the age of 76 years strong!

Born November 20, 1925, the **oldest gymnast** is Johanna Quaas from Germany, who, at the age of 86, was still competing in the amateur competition Landes-Seniorenspiele, staged in Saxony, Germany. She performed a floor-and-beam routine on the set of *Lo Show dei Record* in Rome, Italy, on April 12, 2012, where her record was certified.

The record for **most toilet seats broken with the head in one minute** is 46, achieved by Kevin Shelley on the set of *Guinness World Records—Die größten Weltrekorde* in Cologne, Germany, on September 1, 2007. Pee-yew! Hope he washed his head afterward!

FACT!
Shelley is an elementary school teacher from Indiana and a fourth-degree black belt in Tae Kwan Do.

TOP TOILET FEATS:

The **fastest time to topple 10 portable toilets** is 11.3 seconds and was achieved by Philipp Reiche from Germany on June 22, 2013.

The **fastest marathon dressed as a toilet** is 2 hours, 57 minutes, 28 seconds and was achieved by Marcus Mumford of the UK at the 2014 Virgin Money London Marathon in London, on April 13, 2014.

The **most times to pass through a toilet seat in one minute** is nine and was achieved by Ilker Cevik of Turkey in Milan, Italy, on April 8, 2011.

Not letting age stand in his way, 70-year-old Lee Chin-Yong of South Korea completed the **most consecutive chin-ups**—612—on December 29, 1994. He performed the feat over 2 hours, 40 minutes.

When push comes to shove, Konda Sahadev of India breaks world records! On February 28, 2011, in Hyderabad, he achieved the **fastest time to push a car one mile**: 11 minutes, 39 seconds. The van weighed 5,952 pounds.

HANG IN THERE!
The **longest four-finger hang** is 2 minutes, 26.3 seconds, set by Jörgen Holm of Sweden, on August 31, 2007.

The **fastest time to husk a coconut using the teeth** is 28.06 seconds, achieved by Sidaraju S. Raju of India. On March 30, 2003, he husked a coconut measuring 30.7 inches in circumference and weighing 10 pounds, 6.4 ounces in Bangalore.

You wouldn't want Keshab Swain of India nudging you. On February 29, 2012, he achieved the **most green coconuts smashed in one minute with the elbows**—85.

NUTTY RECORDS:

The **fastest time to pierce four coconuts with a finger** is 12.15 seconds and was achieved by Ho Eng Hui of Malaysia, in Milan, Italy, on April 21, 2011.

The **most coconuts smashed with a baseball bat on a person's head in a minute** is 83, set by Muhammed Rashid of Pakistan, on February 28, 2014.

The **most coconuts smashed with one hand in one minute blindfolded** is 43. Muhamed Kahrimanovic of Bosnia-Herzegovina accomplished this feat on April 6, 2014.

The **most drink cans crushed with the hands in one minute** is 17. René "Golem" Richter of the Czech Republic set the record during the live broadcast of *Das Sommerfest der Abenteuer* in Magdeburg, Germany, on June 2, 2012.

The **fastest time to eat a drinking glass** is 1 minute, 27 seconds, set by Patesh Talukdar of India on March 10, 2011. Do not try this one at home, kids!

The **longest duration holding an iron cross position on Roman rings** is 39.23 seconds, by superstrong gymnast Zak Kerkoulas at Chelsea Piers in New York City, on August 27, 2010. A proper iron cross requires the body to be rigid with arms at a 90-degree angle to the body and parallel to the floor.

The **fastest time to pull a thresher 15 meters** (49 feet, 3 inches) **by a team of 15** is 13.78 seconds, set by Team Thiess at the Kingaroy Showground in Queensland, Australia, during the 2008 Peanut Festival. Threshers are large farm machines weighing thousands of pounds.

The **fastest time to pull a car more than 30 meters** (100 feet) **by mouth** is 18.42 seconds, achieved by Igor Zaripov in Las Vegas, Nevada, on April 12, 2012.

The **most full-contact punch strikes in one hour** is 29,850, by Paddy Doyle at Stamina's Gym, Erin Go Bragh Sports Centre, Erdington, Birmingham, UK, on January 21, 2008.

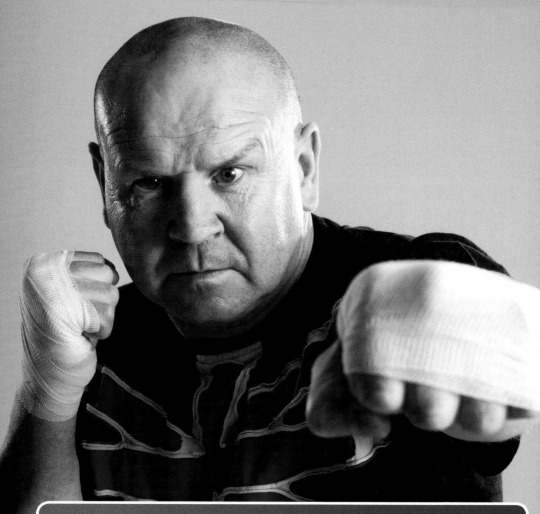

KNOCKOUT RECORDS:

The **most full-contact punch strikes in one minute by a man** is 805, set by Robert Ardito from Australia, on March 18, 2009.

The **most full-contact punch strikes in one minute by a woman** is 556, achieved by Ayaka Miyao from Japan, on May 5, 2011.

The **most punches with one hand in 60 seconds** is 301. Australian Mick Fabar achieved the record on the morning television show *Today*, in Sydney, New South Wales, on November 22, 2011.

Collision safety expert W. R. "Rusty" Haight could offer a crash course on record-breaking! By February 2003, he had endured the **most crash tests in cars**, 718, as a "human crash test dummy," due to his work as a traffic-collision reconstructionist. He teaches law enforcement–accident investigators and engineers about understanding crashes.

The **most times hit by a car in two minutes** is eight, by stuntman Dietmar Loeffler of Germany on the set of *Guinness World Records—Die größten Weltrekorde* in Cologne, on November 23, 2007.

Jay Wheddon is definitely not a morning person! On October 3, 2008, in London, UK, Wheddon broke the record for **most alarm clocks smashed using feet in one minute**—88! Who says you can't stop time?

Steve Schimdt achieved the **most lifts of a 100-kilogram** (220 pound) **weight using the teeth in one minute** on July 13, 2013. He lifted this weight a total of 60 times at the Leslie United Methodist Church in Leslie, Missouri.

The **fastest time to run a half marathon while pushing a stroller** is 1 hour, 30 minutes, 51 seconds, by Nancy Schubring. She achieved the feat at the Mike May Races Half Marathon, Vassar, Michigan, on September 15, 2001.

ACE!

On May 9, 2012, Australian tennis player Samuel Groth recorded the **fastest serve of a tennis ball by a male** at 163.4 miles per hour during an ATP Challenger event in Busan, South Korea. The serve came during Groth's second-round match against Uladzimir Ignatik from Belarus. In the match, Groth also hit serves recorded at 158.9 miles per hour and 157.5 miles per hour. However, Groth still lost the match 6–4, 6–3.

The record for **greatest distance climbed up a pole in an inverted position in one minute** is 31 feet, 11 inches, achieved by Nele Bruckmann of Germany, on September 1, 2007.

The **most weight lifted by barbell upright row in one hour** is 142,859 pounds, 8 ounces. Eamonn Keane of Ireland achieved the feat at Louisburgh Gym in Louisburgh, County Mayo, on July 24, 2012. He managed an astonishing 1,620 repetitions of 88 pounds throughout his attempt.

The **most chin-ups in the human flag position** is 14 and was achieved by Canadian circus artist Dominic Lacasse. Also known as the Flag Man, he accomplished this on the set of *Lo Show dei Record* in Milan, Italy, on July 10, 2014.

The **longest duration to maintain a human flag** is 1 minute, 5.71 seconds. Wang Zhonghua of China achieved the feat on August 15, 2011.

The **longest distance pulled by a horse while on full body burn** is 1,551 feet, 2 inches, by Roland Halápi in Kisoroszi, Hungary, on November 12, 2008.

THIS LITTLE PIGGY . . .

broke a Guinness World Records title! The **heaviest deadlift with the little finger** is 242 pounds, 5 ounces. Armenian Suren Aghabekyan accomplished this feat in Yerevan, on March 23, 2013. He held the weight for 7 seconds.

FINGER FACTS:

The **heaviest weight to be deadlifted by a fingernail** is 19.11 pounds, achieved by Indian Chikka Bhanu Prakash in Hyderabad, Andhra Pradesh, on November 20, 2011.

The **heaviest deadlift using the little fingers** is 148 pounds, 12 ounces, achieved by Kristian Holm from Norway in Herefoss, on November 13, 2008.

The **most finger snaps in one minute** is 278, achieved by Jens Gudmandsen of Sweden in Stockholm, on November 7, 2008.

On February 12, 2012, Neal Hardy of Australia really nailed his world-record attempt. On that date in Canberra, he achieved the record for the **heaviest concrete block break on a bed of nails**. Hardy had 15 blocks, weighing 1,708 pounds, 8 ounces, placed on his chest that were then broken.

Paddy Doyle doesn't skip leg days at the gym. On November 8, 2007, he performed the **most squats in one hour**, 4,708. He felt the burn at Stamina's Boxing Self Defence Gym in Erin Go Bragh Sports Centre, Birmingham, UK.

The **most weight lifted using Atlas stones in one hour** is 30,435 pounds, achieved by Nick Mallory in Hemel Hempstead, UK, on October 28, 2011. Nick lifted the 110-pound-plus stone 275 times.

THINK BIG!

The **heaviest competitive male bodybuilder** was Daniele Seccarecci of Italy, whose competition weight was 297.62 pounds when he was weighed on the set of *Lo Show dei Record* in Rome, on March 18, 2010. Sadly, he passed away in 2013.

The **heaviest competing sportswoman** is Sharran Alexander of London, UK, who weighed 448 pounds on December 15, 2011. Alexander actively competes all around the world as an amateur sumo wrestler and is recognized by the British Sumo Federation in the UK.

The **heaviest living athlete** is sumo wrestler Emmanuel "Manny" Yarborough of Rahway, New Jersey. He stands 6 feet, 8 inches tall and weighs 704 pounds. He was introduced to sumo by his judo coach, and has since ranked number one in the Open Sumo Wrestling Category for Amateurs.

Mark Stretton from the UK recorded the **heaviest longbow draw weight** on August 15, 2004, in Somerset. Stretton drew the longbow, weighing 200 pounds, to the maximum draw on an arrow of 32.5 inches. This large wooden weapon was used by medieval archers.

Asha Rani of India is always happy to lend an ear, even for pulling a car! On June 20, 2013, Rani achieved the record for the **heaviest vehicle pulled using both ears by a female**: 3,747 pounds, 13.74 ounces in Leicester, Leicestershire, UK. She pulled the car a distance of 16 feet, 4.8 inches.

The **heaviest object sword-swallowed** is a Dewalt D25980 demolition hammer weighing 83 pounds, 12 ounces. Thomas Blackthorne from the UK swallowed the 0.94-inch-thick drill bit, and then held the full weight of the hammer and bit for more than three seconds. He accomplished the feat on the set of *Guinness World Records—Die größten Weltrekorde*, in Cologne, Germany, on November 23, 2007. Oh yes, and the hammer was switched on during the attempt!

The **longest time to hold a person above the head, in a standing position on one hand**, is 1 minute, 16.38 seconds, achieved by Markus Ferber and Clarissa Beyelschmidt (both from Germany) on the set of *Lo Show dei Record* in Rome, Italy, on March 11, 2010.

The **heaviest weight lifted by human beard** is 140 pounds, 16 ounces and was achieved by Antanas Kontrimas of Lithuania on the set of *Rekorlar Dünyasi* in Istanbul, Turkey, on June 26, 2013.

Kontrimas also holds the record for **heaviest vehicle pulled by beard**: 4,303 pounds, 6.72 ounces. He set this record in Vilnius, Lithuania, on December 13, 2014.

While performing his world record feat, Wei Shengchu from China was on pins and needles—or, rather, the needles were on him! On June 11, 2013, Shengchu achieved the **most needles inserted into the head**, 2,188, on the set of *Guinness World Records—Rekorlar Dünyasi* in Istanbul, Turkey.

HOLD THAT PLANE!

The **longest time to prevent the takeoff of two Cessna airplanes pulling in opposite directions** is 1 minute, 0.6 seconds. Chad Netherland held on tight and set the record at Richard I. Bong Airport in Superior, Wisconsin, on July 7, 2007.

The record for the **longest time to restrain two cars on inclines**, meanwhile, is 17.36 seconds. Tomi Lotta of Finland achieved this feat on the set of *La Nuit Des Records* in Paris, France, on October 10, 2006.

Lisa Dennis of the UK smashed her way through 923 roof tiles (arranged in stacks of 10) on July 11, 2014, to earn the female record for **most roof tiles broken in one minute**. She also holds the title for **fastest time to break 1,000 roof tiles**: 83.98 seconds.

NO PAIN, NO GAIN!
The **farthest distance to pull a vehicle with meat hooks in the back** is 366 feet, 6 inches, set by Canadian Burnaby Q. Orbax at the Pacific National Exhibition in Vancouver, on October 25, 2011. Burnaby pulled an 8,929-pound truck, which is around the weight of a female African elephant!

Fruit lovers may want to look away now. The **most watermelons smashed with the head in one minute** is 43 and was achieved by German Tafzi Ahmed at the Rose Festival event in Saxony-Anhalt, on May 27, 2011. Now that's using your melon!

The **most full-contact kicks in one hour** is 5,750, by Paddy Doyle on November 8, 2007.

Paddy, often called the World's Fittest Man, certainly keeps himself in tip-top shape. He first became a fitness fan as a member of the British Army's Parachute Regiment. After being discharged, he took up judo, boxing, and gymnastics on his road to becoming an endurance athlete. Paddy has more Guinness World Records than anyone else in the UK! As of July 2014, he had broken 55 records.

He achieved the **most push-ups using the backs of the hands and carrying a 100-pound pack in one minute**, 26, at Stamina's Self Defence Boxing Gym in Birmingham, UK, on January 8, 2012.

The **most one-arm push-ups carrying an 80-pound pack in one minute** is 21, by Paddy on September 8, 2011.

On September 6, 2012, he also completed the **most squats in one minute carrying a 40-pound pack**: 49.

The **most rotations on a vertical rope in one minute** is 13, achieved by aerial performer Brandon Pereyda of the United States on the set of *Guinness World Records—Die größten Weltrekorde* in Cologne, Germany, on November 23, 2007. In the same year, he appeared on *America's Got Talent*.

ROW, ROW, ROW YOUR BOAT . . .

. . . to a Guinness World Records title. The **most ocean rows by one person is eight**, by Simon Chalk, who rowed the Atlantic Ocean, east to west, in teams of two (in 1997), five (in 2007–08), six (in 2013), eight (in 2012 and 2014), and 14 (in 2011). He also rowed the Indian Ocean, east to west, solo (in 2003) and in a team of eight (in 2009). Simon's most recent row left Puerto Morgan, Gran Canaria, on February 10, 2014, and arrived at Port St. Charles, Barbados, on March 15, 2014.

FEEL THE BURN!

The **most squats with 130 kilograms** (286.6 pounds) **in two minutes by a woman** is 29, achieved by Maria Catharina Adriana Strik of the Netherlands in Rome, Italy, on April 4, 2012.

British polar explorer Felicity Aston became the **first woman to ski solo across Antarctica** when she arrived at the Hercules Inlet on the Ronne Ice Shelf on January 23, 2012, after a 1,084-mile journey lasting 59 days. She made the trip from the Ross Ice Shelf—with resupplies—while pulling two sledges and without the support of kites or any other aids to propulsion. She traveled on Nordic cross-country skis, dragging her supplies. She reached the South Pole on December 20, 2011.

ANTARCTICA ACHIEVEMENTS:

On February 20, 1935, Dane Caroline Mikkelsen, the wife of a Norwegian whaling captain, made history by becoming the **first woman to set foot on Antarctica**.

The **fastest and first ever solo and unsupported crossing of the Antarctic continent** was achieved by Børge Ousland, who completed the 1,675-mile trek on January 18, 1997, 64 days after setting out on November 16, 1996.

The **youngest Antarctic trekker** was Norwegian Teodor Johansen, who, at 20 years, 4 months, and 29 days old, successfully traversed Antarctica between November 26, 2011, and January 12, 2012.

Austrian Oliver Gratzer throws everything but the kitchen sink—though that might be a future record for him to consider! On March 18, 2010, on the set of *Lo Show dei Record* in Rome, Italy, Gratzer achieved the record for the **most domestic appliances thrown in one minute**—27 stoves!

The **most chokeslams in one minute** is 34, achieved by Italians Nury Ayachi (aka Kaio), Carlo Lenzoni (aka Charlie Kid), and Mariel Shehi on the set of *Lo Show dei Record* in Rome, Italy, on February 25, 2010. Wrestlers perform a chokeslam by grabbing an opponent's neck, lifting him up, and slamming him to the mat, but this maneuver should only ever be attempted by professionals.

HIGH FIVE HONORS

On June 12, 2013, Wei Wei of China set the record for the **fastest time to pull a car 15 meters** (49 feet, 2.5 inches) **by can suction on hands**: 20.70 seconds. He previously achieved the **fastest time pulling a car over 30 meters** (98 feet, 5.1 inches) **by can suction on hands** with a time of 2 minutes, 21 seconds in 2010.

SECTION THREE:
STAMINA

How long can you hold your breath? In this section, learn about the individuals who dig deep and go the extra mile to earn a world record. . . .

As of April 24, 2013, the **longest ongoing pilgrimage** is 40,235 miles, by Arthur Blessitt, who has been walking on a mission since December 25, 1969. He has visited all seven continents, including Antarctica, having crossed 321 nations, island groups, and territories, carrying a 12-foot-tall wooden cross and preaching from the Bible throughout his journey.

The **first people to row the navigable length of the Amazon River** are Mark de Rond of the Netherlands and Anton Wright from the UK, who embarked from Nauta in Peru on September 13, 2013. They rowed to Macapá in Brazil, and arrived on October 14, 2013.

The **shortest time taken by a female to reach the three extreme points (the Three Poles) of Earth** is 1 year, 336 days. Cecilie Skog of Norway achieved this when she summited Mount Everest on May 23, 2004, reached the South Pole on December 27, 2005, and finally claimed the North Pole on April 24, 2006.

Tomas Lundman of Sweden can hold his head high! He achieved the **longest time heading a soccer ball while seated**: 8 hours, 32 minutes, 3 seconds. Tomas has been showing off his ball skills since he was 11 years old when he performed at a circus.

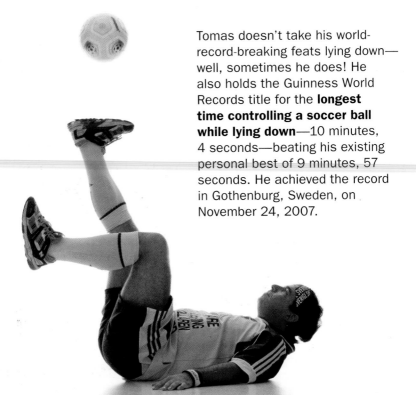

Tomas doesn't take his world-record-breaking feats lying down—well, sometimes he does! He also holds the Guinness World Records title for the **longest time controlling a soccer ball while lying down**—10 minutes, 4 seconds—beating his existing personal best of 9 minutes, 57 seconds. He achieved the record in Gothenburg, Sweden, on November 24, 2007.

The **longest marathon controlling a soccer ball** is 26 hours, achieved by soccer freestyler Dan Magness of the UK in Hong Kong from June 10 to 11, 2010. Without using his hands, Magness kept the ball from touching the ground for the entire attempt.

CHOP TO IT!

On September 19, 2007, Isao Machii of Japan recorded the **fastest time to complete 1,000 cuts of rolled straw mats with a sword**: 36 minutes, 4 seconds. The master swordsman also holds the record for **fastest tennis ball cut by a sword**: the ball was traveling at 440 miles per hour!

On October 15, 2011, Florian Silbereisen of Germany was hot on the heels of a world record. On that date in Chemnitz, he walked the **longest distance over hot plates**: 82 feet, 0.25 inches. OUCH!

Nina Geria of Ukraine is *wheelie* strong! She achieved the **farthest distance to wheelbarrow a car**: 295 feet, 3.3 inches, in Rome, Italy, on March 31, 2012. Geria lifted the back end of the car, while carrying and pushing it the entire distance.

Some people are willing to get on their hands and knees for a world record. Suresh Joachim of Sri Lanka and Canada certainly was. The serial record-breaker crawled for 35.18 miles in Sydney, Australia, from May 18 to 19, 2001, earning himself the title for the **longest continuous crawl**.

INCREDIBLE JOURNEYS:

The **longest barefoot journey** is 924.65 miles. It was taken by Michael Essing of Germany, who traveled from Flensburg to Efringen-Kirchen, between May 30 and September 5, 2013.

The **longest bicycle wheelie journey** is 2,839.6 miles, achieved by Kurt Osburn, who traveled from Hollywood, California, to Orlando, Florida, between April 13 and June 25, 1999.

The **longest journey by bicycle** was more than 402,000 miles, by traveling lecturer Walter Stolle of the UK. He visited 159 countries starting from Romford, UK, from January 24, 1959, to December 12, 1976.

The **longest journey walking backward** goes to American Plennie L. Wingo, who took a 8,000-mile transcontinental walk from Santa Monica, California, to Istanbul, Turkey, between April 15, 1931, and October 24, 1932.

The **longest journey by skateboard** was 7,555 miles and was completed by Rob Thomson of New Zealand. Thomson started in Leysin, Switzerland, on June 24, 2007, and finished in Shanghai, China, on September 28, 2008. That's one gnarly ride!

Want to break the record for the **longest distance swam underwater**? Don't hold your breath! That record belongs to Tom Sietas of Germany. On November 6, 2008, he swam 656 feet, 2 inches with a single breath in Beijing, China.

The **deepest cycling underwater** is 218 feet, 2.11 inches, by Vittorio Innocente of Italy on July 21, 2008. This beat his own record by more than 22 feet.

The **longest duration balancing on four fingers** is a mind-boggling 19.23 seconds, set by the firm-fingered Wang Weibao of China on November 9, 2008. His mighty digits rose to the challenge yet again in 2010, when he snatched the record for **most consecutive "stands" on four fingers**: he managed five in a row.

For most, this record would be too hot to handle, but not Fredrik Karlsson of Sweden. On November 19, 2011, in Stockholm, the fire-breather achieved the **longest duration blowing a continuous fire-flame**, 9.968 seconds.

The **most consecutive pirouettes on a person's head** is four. The feat was achieved by Chinese husband and wife Wei Baohua and Wu Zhengdan on the set of *Lo Show dei Record* in Rome, Italy, on March 28, 2012. Wei wore a cap with a small groove in it for his wife to position her ballet shoe. To successfully complete the record, Wu performed four full rotations on the front of one foot.

The **greatest distance by kayak in 24 hours on flowing water** is 279.02 miles, by Carter Johnson. Carter canoed down the Yukon River starting in Whitehorse, Yukon Territory, Canada, from June 25 to 26, 2011.

Christian Stangl of Austria is the **first person to successfully climb the Triple Seven Summits**—the first, second, and third-highest mountains on all seven continents. He completed the last summit, Shkhara, with an altitude of 17,040 feet on the Georgia-Russia border, on August 23, 2013.

Austrian Walter Geckle is a former Nordic walking world champion, a physical activity using special walking poles. He achieved the record for the **farthest distance Nordic walking in 24 hours**—108.74 miles—in Unzmarkt, Austria, from August 14 to 15, 2010.

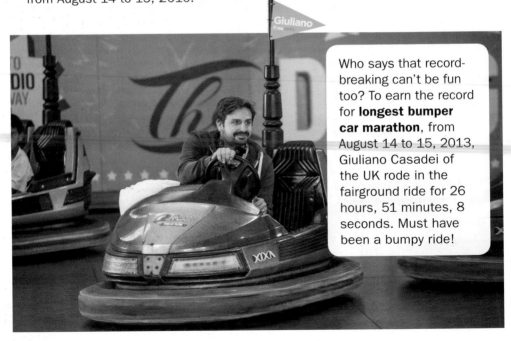

Who says that record-breaking can't be fun too? To earn the record for **longest bumper car marathon**, from August 14 to 15, 2013, Giuliano Casadei of the UK rode in the fairground ride for 26 hours, 51 minutes, 8 seconds. Must have been a bumpy ride!

THREE'S COMPANY!

In September 2009, New Zealand-born sisters Skye Broberg, Nele Siezen, and Jola Siezen set a new **longest time for three contortionists in a box**. The trio climbed into a box with an interior measuring 26 by 27 by 22 inches and remained inside for 6 minutes, 13.52 seconds in Auckland, New Zealand.

THINKING INSIDE THE BOX

One member of the bendy sister act, Skye Broberg, also achieved the **fastest time to cram into a box**, 4.78 seconds, at Melia Whitehouse Hotel, London, UK, on September 15, 2011.

Sam Wakeling of the UK does more on one wheel than most people can do with two! From September 29 to 30, 2007, he traveled the **farthest distance on a unicycle in 24 hours**. He covered 281.85 miles in Aberystwyth, Wales, UK.

Saimaiti Yiming of China is head and shoulders above the rest. He achieved the **farthest distance walking on stilts in 24 hours**, 49.4 miles, walking around Xinjiang, China, from September 30 to October 1, 2003. Yiming also holds the record for walking in the **tallest stilts**—a lofty 55 feet, 10 inches. Must have been a great view.

The **longest duration wingsuit flight** was 9 minutes, 6 seconds, achieved by Jhonathan Florez above La Guajira, Colombia, on April 20, 2012. Florez broke three Guinness World Records over two days for the **greatest absolute** and **greatest horizontal distance covered in a wingsuit flight** and also for the **highest altitude jump**. Wingsuits are specially designed jumpsuits that have extra fabric, or webs, between the arms and legs, allowing fliers to soar like birds. Sadly, Jhonathan passed away in July of 2015.

The **longest belly dance shimmy** was 3 hours, 7 seconds in duration and was achieved by Melanie White of Australia, on February 25, 2012. Belly dancers shimmy by moving their hips or rib cage in a fast, continuous motion.

EXCUSE YOU!

The **longest burp** was 1 minute, 13.57 seconds, by Italian Michele Forgione, also known as Rutt Mysterio, in Reggiolo, Italy, on June 16, 2009.

The **longest concert by a group** lasted 64 hours, 5 minutes, 7 seconds and was achieved by Bodhi Foundation & Maharashtra Youth Development Organization & Group at the "Veterinary Hall" Seminary Hills, Nagpur, India. They performed from April 14 to 16, 2009.

The **longest performance by a solo artist** lasted 501 hours and was achieved by Kuzhalmannam Ramakrishnan of India at Nandavanam Hospital in Kerala, India. He performed from July 5 to 26, 2009. During the same performance, Ramakrishnan also took the record for **longest marathon hand drumming**. After all that drumming, he must have been beat!

Australian Chad Dumble leaves others in his wake. He achieved the record for the **longest continuous wakeboarding marathon**: 6 hours, 42 minutes. Dumble wakeboarded behind a cable tow at Bli Bli Wake Park in Queensland, Australia, on October 9, 2014. He traveled a total distance of 133 miles.

The **longest dance marathon by a team** lasted 24 hours, 1 minute and was achieved at the second MTV O Music Awards at the Roxy Theater in Los Angeles, California, from October 30 to 31, 2011. Team members included Jo Lee, Adrienna Malena, Amber Baker, Kenya Clay, Danielle Rrago, Courteney Winter, Christina Sigler, Marissa Bearer, Amy Morgan, Nichlos Gioioga, Carlee Hoshowski, Melanie Ullman, and Wiii Thomas.

CHA-CHA-CHA-CHA!

On December 2, 2012, the **longest distance danced in a conga line**, 3.41 miles, was achieved by 14 members of staff from the Salford and Stretford Tesco stores at the Manchester United Football Club, Manchester, UK. The conga dancers—all dressed as Santa Claus—completed the challenge in 2 hours, 36 minutes in aid of Manchester United Football Club Foundation's charity.

Matt Wolstenholme of the UK was really on the ball on August 30, 2012. That's the day he set a new record for **longest distance juggling a soccer ball with the feet**: 12.4 miles. Wolstenholme did not drop the ball once throughout the entire attempt.

FOCUS ON: SURESH JOACHIM

In 1969, Arulanantham Suresh Joachim was born in the war-torn city of Jaffna in Sri Lanka, which has inspired him to work toward spreading peace and goodwill around the world. He first found out about Guinness World Records when he acquired a book in 1991. Immediately he felt that this would be a way to gain public attention to promote his charitable ideas. He wants to set up a charity: Universal Fund for Suffering Children. His aim is to become the most prolific record holder in the world and raise $1 billion for charity in the process. The records Suresh wants to break include: **riding a car backward for the farthest distance**, **running backward for the farthest distance**, **riding a motorbike backward the farthest distance**, and **running around the world, through 180 cities, in the shortest time, carrying a peace torch**.

Suresh got off on the right foot—or at least the left foot—in this record attempt. From May 22 to 25, he recorded the **longest duration for balancing on one foot**: 76 hours, 40 minutes, at Vihara Maha Devi Park Open Air Stadium, Sri Lanka. He could not use any support for resting or balancing during this test of stamina.

Suresh achieved the record for the **longest marathon rocking a rocking chair**, from August 24 to 27, 2005, in Ontario, Canada. He rocked on a rocking chair continuously for 75 hours, 3 minutes. To stay awake, he played guitar, read about golf, and had his family present in the room the entire time.

GASP!

This record is sure to take your breath away. The **longest distance swam underwater with one breath in open water** is 492 feet, 1 inch, by Carlos Coste of Venezuela in the Dos Ojos cave system in Quintana Roo, Mexico, on November 3, 2010. Coste's swim lasted 2 minutes, 32 seconds.

The **longest journey swimming in open water** is 3,273.38 miles and was achieved by Martin Strel of Slovenia, who swam the entire length of the Amazon River, from February 1 to April 8, 2007. Hope he didn't meet any piranhas!

The **longest distance kite-surfing in 24 hours** is 401.2 miles and was achieved by Rimas Kinka of Lithuania, off the coast of Islamorada, Florida, on February 26, 2012.

The **greatest distance strapless kite-surfing in six hours** is 105 miles. Petr Pechacek from the Czech Republic set the record off the island of Aruba in 2012.

This record may sting a little. Kanchana Ketkaew from Thailand spent the **longest duration living with scorpions**. She lived in a glass room, measuring 130 by 130 feet, containing 5,320 scorpions for 33 days and nights at the Royal Garden Plaza, Pattaya, Thailand, from December 22, 2008, to January 24, 2009. During the 33 days, she was stung 13 times.

Pollyanna Woodward of the UK jetted into the record books on November 8, 2013, by completing the **longest journey by water jet pack**. Traveling from Gozo Marina in Malta, she circled the island of Como before returning to Malta, while recording the 250th episode of science-tech series *The Gadget Show*. Woodward covered a total distance of 22.64 miles over nearly five hours.

1-2-3!

The **longest hopscotch game** measures 18,064 feet, 3 inches and was created by Step UP 4 Change, Right to Play at the University of Guelph and Free the Children at the University of Guelph in Ontario, Canada, October 1, 2011.

TERRIFIC TREKS:

The **longest journey on crutches** is 3,731.97 miles and was achieved by Guy Amalfitano of France. His journey began on March 16, 2013, and finished on September 6, 2013.

Lars Clausen completed the **longest unicycle journey**—9,125 miles—between April 22 and November 12, 2002. He rode from Tillamook, Oregon, across the country and back to finish in Los Angeles, California, covering 48 states in total.

Husband and wife Phil and Louise Shambrook of the UK completed the **longest tandem bicycle journey**, covering 23,701 miles, departing from Brigg, Lincolnshire, UK, on December 17, 1994, and returning there on October 1, 1997.

The **longest dance marathon by a couple** was performed by Francisco Petatán-Garcia and Joana Salinas-Aviles of Mexico. The couple danced nonstop for an exhausting 35 hours in Acapulco, Guerrero, Mexico, from November 15 to 16, 2008.

On July, 22, 2009, David Slick completed the **longest duration juggling three objects**. He juggled for 12 hours, 5 minutes at the public library in North Richland Hills, Texas. David listened to his MP3 player, which helped him focus on keeping everything airborne. He occasionally sat but stood most of the time.

Don't call Pawan Kumar Srivastava from India a ball hog! He achieved the record for the **longest basketball-dribbling marathon**, 55 hours, 26 minutes, at Lucknow Public College, Lucknow, from December 10 to 12, 2007.

From October 22 to 25, 2009, Aaron Hibbs broke a record that had stood for 25 years! He achieved the **longest Hula-Hooping marathon by an individual using a single hoop**, 74 hours, 54 minutes, in Columbus, Ohio. Who knows? Maybe Hibbs's record will make Hula-Hooping hip again!

The **longest professional wrestling match** lasted 12 hours and was promoted by Shockwave Impact Wrestling as the Ultimate Iron Man Match at the Shelby County Fairgrounds in Sidney, Ohio, on November 6, 2010. The match was contested by American Kickboxer II (aka Brandon Overholser), Dark Angel (aka Mike White), DJ Tom Sharp (aka Tom Crone), Logan Cross (aka Logan Jones), Sid Fabulous (aka Mark Easterday), and "Lightning" Tim Lutz.

Fitness trainer Ronald Sarchian really packs a punch! From June 15 to 17, 2012, he completed the **longest punch-bag marathon**, lasting a record-breaking 50 hours, 9 minutes. It is the fifth Guinness World Records title he has achieved to date.

From August 26, 2002, to January 28, 2003, Andrew Urbanczyk captained the **longest nonstop ocean voyage by a raft**. It took 136 days to sail a straight-line distance of 5,110 nautical miles (5,880 miles) from Half Moon Bay, California, to the Pacific island of Guam.

The **longest mountainboarding race** was the 5th Annual Nate Harrison Grade Race. The race covered 6.95 miles and took place at Palomar Mountain, San Diego County, California, on September 3, 2008.

The **longest open saltwater scuba dive in cold water** is 13 hours, 42 minutes, achieved by Daniel Sammut of Malta on March 19, 2015. During the attempt, Sammut dived to a depth of 36 feet.

In 2006, from August 29 to 30, Croatian Veljko Rogosic found his sea legs. He completed the **longest distance ever swam without flippers in open sea**, 139.8 miles, crossing the Adriatic Sea from Grado to Riccione, Italy.

The **longest paddleboard journey** was 345 miles, completed by Wyatt Werneth, who paddled north up the coast of Florida from May 19 to 27, 2007.

The **longest paddleboard journey by a team** is 32,001 miles from Cape Breton, Canada, to Capbreton in France, a feat achieved by Stephanie Geyer-Barneix, Alexandra Lux, and Flora Manciet (all of France) on August 28, 2009. The journey took 54 days in total.

MORE PADDLEBOARDING RECORDS:

The **farthest distance by stand-up paddleboard in 12 hours on open water** is 80.84 miles, achieved by Chris Bertish of South Africa between Kommetjie and Langebaan, on December 17, 2013.

The **greatest distance on a stand-up paddleboard on flat water in 24 hours by a female** is 90.7 miles, by Robyn Benincasa at Huntington Harbor, Huntington Beach, California, on November 8–9, 2013.

The **fastest crossing of the English Channel by paddleboard** is 5 hours, 9 minutes, set by Michael O'Shaughnessy, on July 18, 2006.

The **longest singing marathon with multiple singers** lasted a staggering 7 days, 5 hours, 47 minutes, and was achieved by the Shree Ramkabir Mandir temple in Carson, California, from July 12 to 19, 2015. Several thousand people attended from several US states and even countries as far away as Panama, and ranged in age from four right up to 86. The singathon centered on traditional Hindu religious songs known as "bhajans."

From March 3 to 7, 2012, in Nagpur, India, Sunil Waghmare achieved the **longest singing marathon by an individual.** The Indian singer performed for 105 hours. He sung a variety of popular Indian songs, and no repeats were allowed within a four-hour period.

The **longest solo ocean row** of 312 days, 2 hours was completed by Erden Eruç of Turkey. He rowed across the Pacific Ocean, east to west, leaving Bodega Bay, California, on July 10, 2007, and finishing at Papua New Guinea on May 17, 2008. The row was part of Eruç's project to travel around the world by human power alone.

Slovenian biker Benka Pulko traveled 111,856 miles on her solo motorcycle journey through 69 countries and all seven continents to secure the **longest motorcycle journey by a woman**. The record-breaking trip started in Ptuj, Slovenia, on June 19, 1997, and ended at the same location 2,000 days later on December 10, 2002.

These guys are never at a loss for words. The **longest speech marathon by a team** is 100 hours and was achieved by Mar Adentro de México, A.C., Toastmasters México—Jalisco and Ayuntamiento de Guadalajara 2010–2012 in Guadalajara, Mexico, from May 18 to 22, 2011.

The **greatest distance traveled on a treadmill in 48 hours** is 251.79 miles. Tony Mangan of Ireland ran from August 22 to 24, 2008, beating the previous record by more than 11 miles.

On October 10, 2010, Craig Pinto achieved the **most football field goals successfully kicked in 12 hours**. He completed a stunning 717 field goals at the Bethpage Football Field in Westbury, New York. In a game, those field goals would add up to 2,151 points.

Craig also achieved the record for the **most football field goals successfully kicked in 24 hours**, 1,000, at Theodore Roosevelt Park, Oyster Bay, New York, on October 9, 2011.

HERE'S A RECORD TO FLIP OVER . . .

The **greatest distance traveled in 24 hours by a team doing cartwheels** is 31 miles. A team of 10 from Beausejour Gymnos completed the feat from September 8 to 9, 2006. They must have been head over heels with their success.

OORAH!
The **fastest marathon in military desert uniform** is 3 hours, 50 minutes, 31 seconds and was achieved by Jennifer Jenks at the Flora London Marathon 2009, in London, UK, on April 26, 2009. Jenks wore standard United Kingdom desert military dress, including shorts, vest, and hat that would be worn in combat zones such as Iraq. She wore running shoes rather than military boots, however.

MARATHON MARVELS:

The **fastest half marathon dressed in full military uniform** is 1 hour, 39 minutes, 40 seconds, achieved by Andy McMahon of the UK at the Inverness Half Marathon in Inverness, UK, on March 11, 2012.

The **fastest marathon in a full military uniform by a man** was also run by Andy McMahon, with a time of 3 hours, 49 minutes, 21 seconds at the Lochaber Marathon, Fort William, UK, on April 19, 2009.

The **fastest marathon in full military uniform by a woman** is 4 hours, 54 minutes, 15 seconds, and was achieved by Sophie Hilaire at the Philadelphia Marathon, Philadelphia, Pennsylvania, on November 22, 2009.

The **fastest cycle across the United States from North to South and West to East** was achieved by Glen Burmeister of the UK in 39 days, 23 hours, 45 minutes from June 25 to August 4, 2012. He started in Sumas, Washington, and finished in New York City.

Reza Pakravan from Iran must have felt the burn in more ways than one in 2011 when he took on the **fastest crossing of the Sahara Desert by bicycle**. He cycled the 1,083-mile route in 13 days, 5 hours, 50 minutes, 14 seconds from March 4 to 17, 2011.

The **fastest marathon carrying a 60-pound pack** was completed in 4 hours, 39 minutes, 9 seconds. Toru Sakurai of Japan ran this record-breaking race at the Tokyo Marathon 2013, on February 24, 2013.

On September 7, 2014, four members of the Nairn Kayak Club achieved the **fastest time to kayak the length of Loch Ness, Scotland, UK**. They crossed the 20.59-mile stretch from Fort Augustus to Dores in 3 hours, 42 minutes, 7 seconds. Wonder if they saw the legendary Loch Ness monster?

SPEEDY SPIDEY!

Spider-Man might be more known for swinging than running, but American Camille Herron earned the female record for the **fastest marathon wearing a superhero costume**—2 hours, 48 minutes, 51 seconds—at the 2012 Route 66 Marathon in Tulsa, Oklahoma. Go, Spidey, go!

South African Nuno Gomes started diving in 1977 and has done over 5,000 dives, more than half of them in caves. His interest in setting the record for the deepest scuba dive began in 1981, when he returned early from a diving trip to the coast because of bad weather. On the first visit to the cave, he dived to only 246 feet. He spent the next 15 years going back and diving in the cave in order to discover its real depth. To accomplish this feat, Nuno had the help of his wife and a team of divers. He also needed to strap seven 19-gallon cylinders weighing 298 pounds to his body. By the end of the dive, he had consumed 12,039 gallons of eight different gas mixtures of air, oxygen, nitrox, and trimix. Even though it took him 20 minutes to get to the bottom of the cave, it took him approximately 11 hours, 30 minutes to surface; this meant that Nuno was underwater for a staggering 12 hours!

On August 23, 1996, Nuno plunged to a depth of 927 feet, 2 inches at the Boesmansgat Cave in the Northern Cape province of South Africa—the **deepest scuba dive in a freshwater cave**. Essentially a very deep sinkhole, the cavern resembles a small lake with vertical sides from the surface.

National swimming star Sertan Aydia of Turkey went for an unusual stroll on April 19, 2015. That's the day he achieved the **longest underwater walk**. He covered 262 feet, 3.24 inches by pacing along the bottom of Anafartalar Olympic Pool in Canakkale, Turkey.

The **longest duration spinning a basketball on the head** is 18.11 seconds, by Mehmet Kekec of Germany at the Soccer Meets Schanze charity event in Hamburg, Germany, on May 28, 2011. Kekec was required to spin a regulation basketball on his finger before transferring the ball to his head, which is when the timer began.

Will Levandowski's rock-climbing skills are solid as, well, a rock. He achieved the **greatest vertical-distance rock climbing in 24 hours**, 29,130 feet, on Flagstaff Mountain near Boulder, Colorado, from May 4 to 5, 2011.

On October 25, 2009, Ashrita Furman stepped up his game. He accomplished the **most stairs climbed while balancing books on the head in one minute**—122! Furman achieved the feat at the Lexington Avenue and 63rd Street New York City subway station.

This Guinness World Records holder is never running on empty. The **greatest average mileage run daily for a single year** is 38.44 miles, achieved by Tirtha Kumar Phani of India, from June 30, 2006, to June 29, 2007, in Calcutta. He ran every day, running 14,031.15 miles in total.

WHO NEEDS ELEVATORS?

Not Kurt Hess of Switzerland. He set the record for the **greatest vertical height ascended by climbing stairs in 24 hours**, 60,974 feet, 4 inches. Hess climbed the Esterli Tower in Lenzburg, Switzerland, 413 times on October 5–6, 2007.

From December 3 to 4, 2007, Mario Trindade of Portugal rode his way into the record books. He achieved the **greatest distance covered by wheelchair in 24 hours** at the Vila Read Stadium by completing 113.34 miles.

WHEELCHAIR WONDERS:

The **fastest time to complete the New York Marathon by a male wheelchair athlete** is 1 hour, 29 minutes, 22 seconds, by Australian Kurt Fearnley, on November 5, 2006.

The **fastest time to complete the London Marathon by a female wheelchair athlete** is 1 hour, 46 minutes, 2 seconds, by American Tatyana McFadden, on April 21, 2013.

The **longest wheelchair basketball marathon** is 27 hours, 32 minutes, achieved by South West Scorpions Wheelchair Basketball Club at Filton College in Bristol, England, from August 11 to 12, 2012.

This next record should be called the hottest thing on snow. The **greatest distance traveled Nordic skiing**, also known as cross-country skiing, in 24 hours is 269.34 miles, achieved by Teemu Virtanen of Finland, from November 16 to 17, 2010.

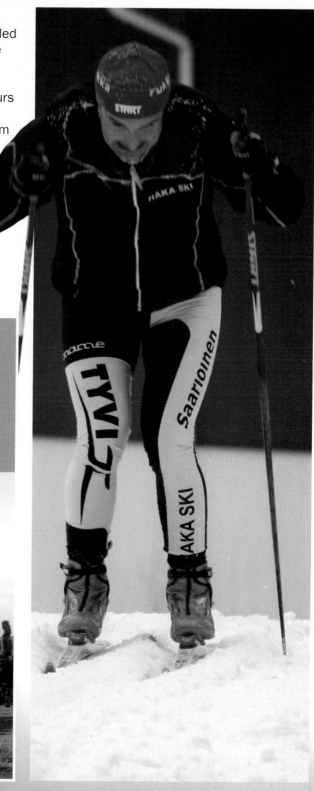

BOING!

Nothing keeps Ashrita Furman from bouncing back. He achieved the **greatest distance on a pogo stick while juggling—** 4 miles, 30 feet—on Easter Island, Chile, in 2010.

After this world-record attempt, Stephen Shanabrook didn't have anything left to spare. He achieved the **longest marathon tenpin bowling** in 134 hours, 57 minutes. From June 14 to 19, 2010, Shanabrook completed 643 games during his "bowlathon" at Plano Super Bowl in Plano, Texas.

The **longest note held on a didgeridoo** is 65.66 seconds, achieved by Lachlan Phelps from Australia, on November 14, 2012. A didgeridoo is a traditional long wind instrument created by indigenous Australians.

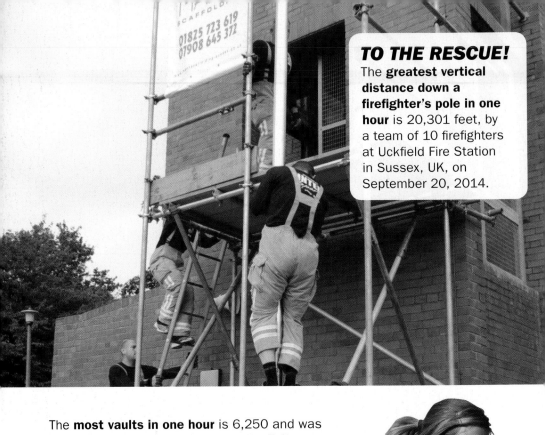

TO THE RESCUE!
The **greatest vertical distance down a firefighter's pole in one hour** is 20,301 feet, by a team of 10 firefighters at Uckfield Fire Station in Sussex, UK, on September 20, 2014.

The **most vaults in one hour** is 6,250 and was achieved by 10 members of the Blue Falcons Gymnastic Display Team at the Meadows Shopping Centre, in Essex, UK, on September 5, 2009.

On February 7, 2009, Eileen Wysocki went for a walk at the Sunlight Mountain Resort in Glenwood Springs, Colorado, and didn't stop until the next day. By then she had covered 25,534 feet—the **most vertical feet uphill in 24 hours by a female wearing snowshoes**.

Wysocki wasn't the only one heading up the slopes at the Sunlight Mountain Resort on February 8, 2009. Dina Mishev was taking on a record of her own: the **greatest distance skied uphill by a woman**. She traveled a snow-tacular 33,044 feet.

Trick-roper Andrew Rotz achieved the **most consecutive Texas skips**—11,123—at the National Convention of the Wild West Arts Club in Las Vegas, Nevada, on March 11, 2003, smashing the previous record set at 4,011. The attempt took 3 hours, 10 minutes to complete.

The **most countries visited by bicycle in seven days** is 11 and was achieved by Glen Burmeister, who cycled from the Czech Republic to Albania, from April 29 to May 5, 2013. Burmeister cycled 979.1 miles through the following countries in 6 days, 11 hours, 53 minutes: Czech Republic, Austria, Slovakia, Hungary, Slovenia, Croatia, Romania, Serbia, Bosnia and Herzegovina, Montenegro, and Albania.

The **most consecutive boxing rounds** is 123 and was achieved by Irish boxer Gerry Cronnelly at the Raheen Woods Hotel in Athenry, County Galway, Ireland, on October 20, 2012. Cronnelly duked it out with 42 competitors!

There's nothing mini about this GWR achievement! The record for the **most holes of miniature golf played by an individual in 24 hours** is 4,729 and was set by David Pfefferle from May 28 to 29, 2008. Over the *course* of the day, he raised $6,000 for charity.

The **most underwater rope jumps in one hour while scuba diving** is 1,608, achieved by Ashrita Furman, at the Aquario de São Paulo, in San Paulo, Brazil, on March 15, 2012.

The **most consecutive skateboard frontside ollies in a halfpipe** is 348 and was set by Keith Baldassare in Merritt Island, Florida, on September 20, 2008. Baldassare started skating at seven years old and now has his own skate park in his backyard.

On October 25, 2004, South African Verna van Schaik plunged to a depth of 725 feet in the Boesmansgat cave in South Africa's Northern Cape province. This feat set a new record for the **deepest scuba dive by a female**. The dive lasted 5 hours, 34 minutes, of which only 12 minutes were spent descending.

The **greatest distance on a human-powered vehicle in 24 hours** is 647 miles, and was achieved by Canadian Greg Kolodziejzyk at Redwood Acres Raceway in Alberta, on July 18, 2006. He set the record in a modified recumbent bicycle, shaped like a bullet to improve aerodynamics.

A relay team of 20 Finnish men swam a record 114.95 miles in 24 hours at the Mäkelänrinteen Swimming Center, Helsinki, Finland, from September 16 to 17, 2005. This bettered the previous **greatest distance relay swimming in 24 hours** by just over a mile.

When push comes to shove, you can certainly count on Aleksandar Chekorov and Aleksandar Smilkov from Macedonia. They hold the record for the **farthest distance pushing a car in 24 hours by a pair**, after moving a Daewoo Matiz 59.07 miles from December 13 to 14, 2014. The vehicle weighed in at 1,896 pounds.